THE POWER

Of A Tear

CORRINE E. MCCRAY

THE POWER

Of A Tear

CORRINE E. MCCRAY

NVP

NUVISION PUBLISHING

To schedule a workshop or conference or to order books, contact us by email at info@gracefullyled.com.

ISBN: 978-1-7343614-0-7 (Paperback)

Published by
NuVision Designs
Wilmington NC
www.nuvisiondesigns.biz/publications

Printed in the United States of America.

DEDICATION

To my big sister/momma (Doris L. Fooks), who inspires me to be true to myself and like our mother does not cry. I have never seen you cry but once heard you cry. It filled my heart with joy to hear you release. I pray you become overwhelmed and your tears freely flow like a river rushing over sand and stones to cleanse your soul and smooth out the afflictions you have endured. May you be renewed and find freedom through the Power of Your Tears.

To my husband, my angel (Ronnie L. McCray) whose enthusiasm to see me grow and cheerleading support enables me to become. I love you for helping me release my gifts and talents. Your joy is my inspiration.

FOREWORD

What a powerful book! From this book I learned growing up is a process. Even though I am a mature man, I am still growing up. **The Power of A Tear**, let me know it's okay to cry; it's okay to show my emotions when I am hurting on the inside. When I cry, it's okay because I am honestly expressing my feelings and emotions. I believe, **The Power of A Tear,** will be a blessing to all who read it. You will discover you are actually located in yourself, and will gain the freedom to express your emotions. Most men do not like to express their feelings and will restrain from publicly shedding a tear. Crying cleanses the soul, and allows us to look within. This book will open your soul, and renew your mindset. Over the years I've noticed the power and insight God has invested in my wife. In this season she is destined to be a blessing to His people. Corrine has always had a heart for God's people who are trying to find their way. If you read this book with an open heart, you will realize **The Power of A Tear,** is more effective than counseling.

Dr. Ronnie L. McCray

ENDORSEMENTS

Corrine McCray's, *"The Power of A Tear"* details the importance of shedding tears for our maximum benefit with such a warmth and clarity that you are compelled to its instructions.

I met Corrine while we both pursued our Life Coaching credentials. She has a special calling and I am thrilled to recommend this gentle, guiding outlook on tears that she presents. Her espousal on the subject is authentic and personal. She does an excellent job describing how our tears shape who we are and how we relate to ourselves.

I would definitely say my colleague has penned an excellent, easy read but one that is also very thoughtful and inspirational.

Joyce M. Barr, CLC, CPM, MPA, CLP - Panama City, Panama

Minister Corrine McCray has opened such a healing revelation of one of the least talked about gifts our creator blessed us with. She reveals from the heart of God *"The Power of A Tear"* as she write from her personal journey.

I was blessed as I read page fifteen, she writes "your strength has been renewed through your tears". What a powerful word of life and encouragement.

Corrine is a Committed Woman of God, a Life Bearing Force and a Sister to all that embrace her for the Vessel that she is and draw from the well of treasures that she has been entrusted with for the building of the Kingdom of our God.

This book, *"The Power of A Tear"* will definitely open another road to freedom when we need a release. She states in her own language the purpose of Tears in both seasons of Joy and Sorrow. They are a gift to be used when needed, for they (TEARS) express directly to the heart of God the words that we can't express in depth. Read this short well written and inspiring book with an open heart and mind; be blessed and pass it to someone you love.

Dr. Mae Tuggle
Pastor, Harvest Time Family Ministries, Wallace
NC

TABLE OF CONTENTS

INTRODUCTION
Ask Anything of Me

I am blessed to be at a great season in my life, my sixties. As I write that opening sentence I am laughing at myself. You see, for years I would never give my true age. Yes, I always claimed to be 3-5 years younger than my actual age. I'll never forget an incident when I was asked my age and couldn't remember. My cousin laughed stating, "You've lied so long about your age you can't remember how old you are". I laughed with her but I was also dismayed at the truth. Even worst, I was only in my thirties, still a baby. I believe it had something to do with my childhood imagination and proclamations inspired by Walt Disney characters like Peter Pan, "I'll never grow up. I'll always be a child". And, Jiminy Cricket, "I'm gonna live to be 103". I had conditioned my mind to never growing old and living a long life. This belief was sealed by my Biblical upbringing and teachings. God promised us a long life if we honored our parents. Our Biblical patriarchs lived up to 900 years old. The Father created man to live for eternity and I was gonna do just that! Still today I proclaim, "I'm gonna fly (referring to the Biblical rapture teachings) not die".

Now, blessed to be in my sixties the focus is 'Quality of Life' and 'Happiness'. Recently, I felt sadness in my heart. Now, I never ignore feelings of sadness because my desire and goal is to be happy. I began to search for the reason for my sadness. In doing so, became aware of conversations with loved one and noticed the bitterness and anger in their words and yes, in their hearts. I realized in the winter season of their lives (ages 60+) they were terribly unhappy. Early in my childhood I realized 'unhappiness' is a poison that will slowly eat you alive. The symptoms are undetectable because people tend to 1) substitute things trying to cure the problem; 2) become a chameleon faking happiness; 3) aspire to be successful to fill the void; and/or 4) believe the joy of the Lord is their strength.

I did my 'go to' remedy and began talking to the Father about my concern for the bitterness and anger in the hearts of those I loved. His answer to me: "Corrine, you know why you are not angry or bitter? Before I could even answer He said, "Because you cried. Now, let me tell you about the "Power of A Tear".

"When you cry you release the negativity that is trying to attach itself to your spirit and cause you harm. When you cry you move the heart of the

Father and He sends help. When you cry and a tear falls into the corner of your mouth what do you taste? I replied, salt. He said, you are releasing the stress thru sodium that can cause high blood pressure. When you cry so hard that snot runs from your nose, you release mucus blockage or backup that affects the eyes, ears, nose and throat functioning. When you cry so hard that you fall asleep like a baby, then, you have truly cast your cares upon me, you sleep sound and when you awake it's all over. Your strength has been renewed through your tears and you have laid your burden down at my feet."

Truth being told, I have always cried. I cry when I'm happy. I cry when I'm sad. I cry harder when other people don't know they need to cry. As the lyrics of an old gospel hymn states, "I cried and He delivered me. He delivered my poor soul." I've been called a cry baby, sensitive, too compassionate, and a punk. But STILL, I CRY!

The Father created us with emotions. Could we be denying ourselves the benefits of His perfect design by shunning, disqualifying and hiding our emotions? Could we be making ourselves gods thinking WE have the power and control of our minds and bodies? There is a level of mind control that is witchcraft and there is a righteous mindset, which is to have the mind of Christ.

1
Emotions, A Special Gift

Positive emotions may be considered as any feeling where there is a lack of negativity, such that no pain or discomfort is felt. The ten most common positive emotions are: joy, gratitude, serenity, interest, hope, pride, amusement, inspiration, awe and love.

Negative emotions can be described as any feeling which causes you to be miserable and sad. These emotions make you dislike yourself and others, and take away your confidence. Emotions that can become negative are: hate, anger, jealousy, guilt, fear, revenge, greed, superstition, shame and sadness.

Let's talk about tears. What are tears? They are fluid that lubricates the eye, and help to keep it clear of dust. Tear fluid contains 12 elements: water, mucin, lipids, lysozyme, lactoferrin, lipocalin, lacritin, immunoglobulins, glucose, urea, sodium and potassium.

What causes tears? Various things like dust, coughing, and yawning to name a few. But we're focusing on one type of tear – emotional tears. It all starts in the cerebrum, where sadness is registered. The endocrine system is then triggered to release hormones to the ocular area, which causes tears to form. Humans shed tears in response to a range of emotions. These tears contain a higher level of stress hormones than other types of tears.

We may choose to suppress our tears thinking they show weakness but, science suggest, it's good to shed a few tears and there are benefits from crying. Researchers have found that crying:

1. Has a soothing effect and self-soothing is an individual regulating their own emotions; calming themselves; reducing their own distress;
2. Crying activates the parasympathetic nervous system (PNS), which helps people relax;
3. Get support from others around them. It is primarily an attachment behavior, and rallies support from people around us.
4. Helps to relieve pain by releasing oxytocin and endorphins, chemicals that make people feel good and also ease both physical and emotional pain. Crying can help reduce pain and promote a sense of well being;
5. Mood Enhancer – crying may help lift people's spirit and make them feel better;
6. Releases toxins and relieves stress. When

we cry in response to stress, our tears contain a number of stress hormones and other chemicals. Crying could reduce the levels of these chemicals in the body, which could, in turn, reduce stress;

7. Aids sleep – crying can help babies sleep better. The calming, mood-enhancing, and pain-relieving effects of crying may help a person fall asleep more easily;

8. Fights bacteria – crying helps to kill bacteria and keep the eyes clean as tears contain a fluid called lysozyme which has powerful antimicrobial properties. It could even help to reduce risks presented by bio-terror agents, such as anthrax.

9. Improves vision – basal tears, which are released every time a person blinks, help to keep the eyes moist and prevent mucous membranes from drying out. The National Eye Institute explains, the lubricating effect of basal tears helps people to see more clearly. When the membranes dry out, vision can become blurry.

Food for thought: The Power of A Tear -- If you choose to dry out your eyes by holding back tears, then you can risk blurring your spiritual vision.

<u>2</u>
Wisdom and Insight

What does the Bible say about tears? Tears are mentioned 36 times in the Bible. Let's look at a few scriptures and examine the Biblical effects of tears or God's response to our tears.

2 Kings 20:5 – "Turn again, and tell Hezekiah the captain of my people, Thus saith the Lord, the God of David thy father, I have heard thy prayer, I have seen thy **tears**: behold, I will heal thee: on the third day thou shalt go up unto the house of the Lord". **(*Tears move God*).**

Job 16:19-20 – "Also now, behold, my witness is in heaven, and my record is on high. My friends scorn me: but mine eye poureth out **tears** unto God". **(People tell you not to cry. That is a contradiction of God's design. Our tears are meant for Him and between us and Him).**

Psalms 6:6 – "I am weary with my groaning; all the night make I my bed to swim; I water my couch with **tears**". **(King David, whom God says is a man after His own heart cried all night long. This great, brave and mighty king cried. So, why do we** *deceive ourselves in believing we are strong because we don't cry)?*

Psalms 42:3 – "My **tears** have been my meat day and night, while they continually say unto me, 'Where is thy God?' " (*Again, our tears are to our God).*

Psalms 56:8 – "Thou tellest my wanderings: put thou my **tears** into thy bottle: are they not in thy book"? (*God thinks so much of our tears He places them in a book of permanence and remembrance because they speak our truth louder than words).*

Psalms 126:5 – "They that sow in **tears** shall reap in joy". (*Glory to God, what a promise; and, all because you cried. Hallelujah!!)*

Acts 20:31 – "Therefore watch, and remember, that by the space of three years I ceased not to warn every one night and day with **tears**". (*It hurts the true prophet of God to warn people and give them truth).*

Luke 7:44,47 – "And he turned to the woman, and said unto Simon, Seest thou this woman? I entered into thine house, thou gavest me no water for my feet: but she hath washed my feet with *tears*, and wiped them with the hairs of her head"… "Wherefore I say unto thee, her sins, which are many, are forgiven; for she loved much: but to whom little is forgiven, the same loveth little". *(Tears opened the door of forgiveness).*

Revelation 7:17 – "For the Lamb which is in the midst of the throne shall feed them, and shall lead them unto living fountains of waters: and God shall wipe away all *tears* from their eyes". *(When all is said and done, God Himself will wipe the tears from our eyes. Our tears are to help us endure the pains of this world. God knows we will shed them until He wipes them away. Thank you Father).*

<u>3</u>
Tears, Our Saving Grace

As stated earlier, tears help us get support from others around us. You may be familiar with the Biblical characters I am about to mention. If not, please take time to read the scriptures concerning them to aide in your understanding of this chapter. As you read these scriptures you may find yourself moved becoming teary eyed about their situations. As their hearts were broken, expressed through their tears, your heart may feel their sorrow and be moved to tears.

The story of Hannah (1 Samuel 1:2-22). Hannah's name means grace. As indicated in the scriptures, Hannah was:

- Barren – incapable of producing offspring;
- She was the favorite wife of Elkanah;
- Her adversary (Peninnah, Elkanah other wife) provoked her continually;
- She fasted, *wept* and prayed before the Lord year after year without an answer;
- Her husband sought to comfort and support her;
- She finally became desperate and prayed through to an answer by bitterness of soul

(anger and disappointment of being treated unfairly), *weeping* and making a vow;
- She prayed so long, *weeping* so hard she disturbed the High Priest, who annoyed accused her of being drunk;
- In response to her **tears** and verbal expression of sorrow, the High Priest spoke a blessing into her life;
- Her prayer was heard, she conceived and bore a son. Not just one son, her womb was opened and she conceived 5 more times. *ALL BECAUSE SHE CRIED!!!*

The story of Jeremiah, the weeping prophet (Jeremiah 14:17).
- A young man set apart by God to be a messenger to the nations of Israel;
- For forty years he warned the people about the doom that would befall them if they continued in their sinful ways;
- He was commanded to give this message to Judah – 'that **tears** should be permitted to run from his eyes day and night without ceasing, for the calamity that was to come upon them;
- For years continually both day and night he

cried on behalf of the people;
- The burden, the grief, the pain he knew was to befall the people could no longer be expressed in words;
- The weight and depth of their doom could only be expressed through **tears** of sorrow, anguish and dismay;
- It hurts the true prophet of God to warn people and give them truth. ***HE CRIED FOR THEM.***

The story of our Lord and Savior, Jesus Christ (John 11:28-35; Luke 19:41-44; Hebrews 5:7):
- Arriving at the home of his friends seeing Mary who had lost her brother (Lazarus) along with family and friends crying, Jesus *wept* in response to their grief.
- Jesus also *wept* because he too loved Lazarus
- He *wept* over Jerusalem predicting its overthrow. Again, true prophets hurt and cry for the people who understand not what they do.
- He *wept* while offering prayers and supplications (action of asking or begging for something earnestly or humbly) for the

people.
- Jesus expressed all the humanity and emotional feelings we have. While on earth he *cried* with and for people.

ARE WE ABOVE OUR PERFECT EXAMPLE, JESUS, WHO WEPT?

4
Dear Brethren

My brother, my brother! Jesus, the anointed Messiah who was beat all night long with a cat-o-nine tails whip, and the hairs from his beard were ripped off his face. A man just like you, endured brutal beatings, and the records states during it all 'He opened not his mouth'. Jesus didn't yell or scream out in pain and anguish as He was being physically abused. Yet, this same man in response to His love ones sorrow and the lost of His friend, Lazarus WEPT. Jesus released His emotions through His tears. Our Lord and Savior did not think it a mockery against his manhood to cry before family and friends.

King David, a mighty warrior was praised in song by the women for killing 10,000 men in battle. He gained notoriety as a young lad for boldly standing up to a giant who was intimidating the King and his army. This giant named Goliath challenged to fight anyone daring to oppose him. Lil David without hesitation stepped forward questioning Goliath for thinking he could come against God's chosen people. Refusing to wear military armor Lil David (under 6' tall) swiftly killed the giant (over 9' tall) and cut off his head.

This bold, unrelenting warrior who pursued his enemies and fought battle after battle came to a place in his life when he simply couldn't take it anymore. Exhausted from battles; tired of looking over his shoulder; and continuously having his life threatened even though innocent of any wrong doing, curled up on his sofa and cried all night long. He made a permanent record of shedding tears and expressing his emotions through the Psalms he wrote, and expressed his sorrows in song and musical instruments. David was not ashamed to release his emotions or to share them with the world. He found his truest strength was in the expressing of his heart. In his moments and seasons of anguish David wrote:

- "I am weary with my groaning; all the night make I my bed to swim; I water my couch with my tears (Palms 6:6)".
- "My tears have been my meat day and night, while they continually say unto me, Where is thy God? (Psalms 42:3)".

David cried so much he posed a question to God:

- "Thou tellest (count or take account) my wanderings: put thou my tears in thy bottle: *are they not in thy book?"* (Psalms 56:8)

Knowing God was moved by his tears David proclaimed:

- "They that sow in tears shall reap in joy (Psalms 126:5)".

Confirming David's claim to reaping joy from tears, when King Hezekiah was sick unto death God sent him a message through the Prophet Isaiah:

- "Go, and say to Hezekiah, thus saith the Lord, the God of David thy father, I have heard thy prayer, I have seen thy tears: behold, I will add unto thy days fifteen years (Isaiah 38:5)".

Dealing with the hardships facing his people, the children of Israel, Jeremiah, a prophet wrote:

- "Oh that my head were waters, and mine eyes a fountain of tears, that I might weep day and night for the slain of the daughter of my people (Jeremiah 9:1)".
- "But if you will not hear it, my soul shall weep in secret places for your pride; and mine eye shall weep sore, and run down with tears, because the Lord's flock is carried away captive (Jeremiah 13:17)".

The Apostle Paul expressed the joy the people of

Corinth gave him during his struggles:

- "For out of much affliction and anguish of heart I wrote unto you with many tears; not that ye should be grieved, but that ye might know the love which I have more abundantly unto you (2 Corinthians 2:4)".

Apostle Paul speaking on Esau shedding tears in his brokenness:

- "For ye know how that afterward, when he (Esau) would have inherited the blessing, he was rejected: for he found no place of repentance, though he sought it carefully with tears (Hebrews 12:17)".

During his overwhelming trials, Job in one day lost his children, livestock, livelihood and physical health. But it was a condemning visit from his friends that made him state:

- "My friends scorn me: but mine eye poureth out tears unto God (Job 16:20)".

My brothers, dealing with the circumstances of life can be difficult and a life threatening challenge. Your Father, the Most High, knows the challenges and obstacles you will face. He knows that His enemy is out to kill, steal from and destroy His greatest creation MAN. His book, the Holy Bible, addresses every life situation and provides insight through the lives of those before us. Their examples both good and bad, right and wrong, are for our benefit and self examination. The records of the men above was written to let you know it's okay to cry when you are uncertain, heavy laden, tired, confused, overwhelmed, in pain and anguish, sorrowful or joyful.

Subjecting yourself to the strain of withholding tears puts you at the slow risk of dying from high blood pressure; becoming disabled from a stroke and/or at a higher risk of cutting your life short through heart attack.

Dearest brothers, truth be told you have been duped (deceived, tricked) by the idea real men don't cry. You have been manipulated by a falsehood concerning your emotions. It takes strength to release the truth of your emotions. It takes much more strength to stand strong despite your emotions. Women, like the Father, are moved by inner strength; your ability to express the truth of your heart.

Show me a man that can cry and I'll show you a man who can wipe the tears from my eyes. Like the Father, this man is able to bare my sorrows and grief because he can feel my heart and in his strength soothe my fears.

5
Dear Sisters

Beautiful sisters, my lady and heart to heart friend, you likewise have been robbed of your glory in so many ways. Rest assured the Father is aware and mindful of His daughters. We are precious jewels in His kingdom. He created us in His image and likeness. He blessed us with a big heart full of love, the essence of Him. Our unique spirit has, will and continues to be capable of withstanding the struggles, hardship and injustices. Yet, despite our stories, and our journeys we are anointed with a heart that loves and loves again, without judgment. Our great capacity to love musters the strength to have faith and hope.

The first man Adam was instructed to protect the garden. The love of a woman is so powerful she will willingly die to protect her family and loved ones. Her personal life is the least of her concerns always putting the family first.

Unfortunately, and against the design of the Creator, one of our greatest challenges has been our femininity. Too often we find ourselves thinking our femininity is a blessing and a curse. We are blessed with the beauty of our physical form and the ability to nurture through our embrace; heal with a hug or a kiss; and assure emotional security in our arms. The love from a woman can build up, strengthen, encourage and help create vision through dreams we nurture.

The notion of our femininity being a curse does not so much stem from the curse of painful childbirth due to the fall of man in the garden, but from the continual threat of being violated both physically and emotionally.

Yes, we know the worldwide history of injustice and abuse. For too many generations of diaspora we have been forced and given no choice but to step into the role of man. Too often finding ourselves alone without a man for various reasons, some not of our own making: incarceration, homosexuality, immature males, insecure/fearful males, homicide, police brutality, divorce, health issues, etc. African American women have the additional challenge of other ethnic groups of women who seek relationships with African American men. Many African American women are alone not by choice or homosexual preference but because they remain loyal to their God given counterpart, the African American male who finds favor with another.

The continual fight to be acknowledged as the precious jewels the Father created and designed us to be experiencing loneliness, emotional/physical abuse, rejection, and other negativity, we can become bitter, harsh and find ourselves refusing to cry. It is heartbreaking when a delicate flower becomes brittle. It is against the nature of femininity to withhold love and suppress emotions. To do so, is to allow the adversary of our Father (Satan) to control our hearts and minds. If you want to defeat Satan and his imps, flourish in the image of the Father and express the fullness of His great love. The Father will always uphold and prosper those who abide by His laws and statutes. So my dearest sisters, strive to be who the Father designed you to be, loving, caring, nurturing, kind and beautiful. Stay true to His purpose for your life and allow the all knowing, righteous judge to avenge you.

6
After You Cry

Tears usually mean we've lost control. We can no longer take the pressure. We can no longer ignore the pain. We can no longer hide our feelings, and the tears are released.

So, what do we do after we cry, after we shed tears? It's our choice. Some choose to be angry, staying mad at the person or the cause of their pain and their tears. Some choose to become bitter. To hide the pain in their heart and seal it in their mind vowing to never forgive or forget what has been done to them causing them so much pain. Some choose to continue crying and never let go of the sadness. Some choose to hold onto the pity, delighting in the attention of the empathy others feel or show towards them. All of these are negative responses. A trap designed to lock you in a state of a hardened heart or to leave you so weakened you have no strength to withstand future obstacles.

Others choose to get up, wash their face, take a deep breath and begin again. Others choose to wash their face, dry their eyes, think about what caused the pain, then consider the part they have played enabling them to identify their options so they can make things better.

The Bible lets us know in Psalms 30:5, "For his anger endureth but a moment; in his favour is life: weeping may endure for a night, but joy cometh in the morning". It's our choice. To decide to let go is the choice to release the pain. It's okay, one of the Father's methods of healing is to cry it out. Let the tears flow so you can stand strong and face a new day.

Ask yourself the question. After I have cried, after I have shed my last tear, what do I do now? Do I stay in the place of sorrow and grief? Do I move on? Do I go backwards? Do I choose to forget acting like nothing really happened? There is grave danger in blocking out, hiding, ignoring and/or convincing ourselves our pain is not real. If it hurt enough to make you cry, the experience was real. I believe part of the reason for the bitterness and anger in the loved ones I mentioned in the beginning is due to the suppression of their true feelings, needs, and the inability to express their emotional pain. Their silent response to the selfish, abusive, inconsiderate spirits of others gave room for continual emotional pain.

My sensitivity caused me to easily shed tears and to cry out. The pain in my heart was felt so strongly I had to let people know when they were hurting me and because the pain was in my heart often I had to explain how they were hurting me. As a child, I could not understand how God was love yet, sometimes the actions of His people was harsh, cruel and unloving. I did not understand how people could ignore my emotional tears. Now, I was not a cry baby trying to manipulate and have my way. I was one who felt the harsh words and the rejection of my emotional needs like a sharp knife piercing my heart. My outcry, "you're hurting me", was so I could be heard and understood.

From my outcry I learned that the Father hears me and I learned to hear His voice. Just as His Word promises, when I cried He reached down to console me. He would explain to me in a sweet soothing voice why I felt what I felt. He taught me that discipline was good and necessary but all we do must be done in love for it to be effective. He showed me how He studies each individual so He can help them develop strong character, faith and commitment to His voice. I learned to take my cares first to God my Father so He could guide me ensuring positive outcomes. The Father revealed the humanity of man so I would understand we are all subject to error. When I was wrong He corrected me showing the cause and effect of my actions. He trained me to look beyond what I hear, see or feel and focus on the intent of the heart. I learned to identify when someone truly meant me harm versus when someone had the best of intentions but erroneous methods.

He taught me to let Him be the judge and avenger of wrong doings. When I talked to Him about a situation if He said I needed to change, I learned to submit myself to His instructions. If He said my heart and motives were pure, I knew I was free to let go of the pain that was caused by evil intent knowing He would correct the situation. There is nothing more powerful then the Father saying, He finds no fault in you. And there is nothing more frightening then to know the Father is not pleased when men wrongfully use or abuse His children.

So, what do you do after you have cried and shed your last tear? I believe if you surrender your emotions to the Father, you will receive clarity and understanding. As stated in Chapter One, the lubricating effect of basal tears helps people to see more clearly. You have to shed the tears in order to receive clarity. Now, that things are clear what do you do?

7
Now What?

I wish I could provide a formula or a step by step procedure to outline and direct your next steps. I believe we've become too reliant upon such teachings and course of action. If we're honest with ourselves, we'll admit the disappointment we felt when we tried someone else's method only to realize it does not work for us.

Our emotions are a gift from the Most High. Emotions are designed to help us balance our heart and mind. Tears are the flow of fluid releasing overwhelming ecstasy or intense pressure. One tear drop is so precious to the Father that He places them in a bottle of remembrance. I don't know how true this is, but I've read and have, been told, the Father turns dried tears into jewels.

One of the benefits of shedding tears is receiving clarity. The question is what do we do once we have clarity? This clarity is seeing our true selves. Reflecting on the reason we cry equips us to investigate and examine ourselves. The best way to self examine is through the eye of the Father. You now know what made you cry. You understand your reaction to the pain or to the joy. Positive tears shed in reaction to joy and happiness needs only to be responded to with gratefulness. A thankful heart for the joy experienced. Negative tears require more serious thought or consideration. As you shed these tears did you feel hurt, anger, confusion, frustration, bitterness, abused, rejected, revengeful? The ability to connect your mind with your emotions is the clarity needed to appropriately deal with the situation(s) which caused you to cry. The antidote can only be found through your relationship with the Spirit of the Most High. We can spend time and money talking to a professional. The technique they use is probing, asking question after question in search of a clue to connect your emotions with a cause. Seeking professional help is good and proven to be helpful. As a Life Coach, I realize the importance and impact of face to face interaction and the comfort of talking through issues with someone you can trust. When the Father created man He stated, it is not good for man to be alone. We need one another. A trusting, insightful ear is a blessing.

The wisest and most effective ear to seek is that of the Holy Spirit. The third person of the Godhead's role is to be our comforter; to bring back to our remembrance all things; to give us knowledge and understanding; to help us see our truth; and to help us design a remedy. You may have heard people say, get to the root of the problem. The Holy Spirit is aware of the root cause of every situation and at one with the Father, knows just how much you can bear. Full of wisdom and the love of the Father, the Holy Spirit gently works with us until we become aware or conscious of something and/or come to realize or understand.

I stated seeking the Holy Spirit is the wisest choice because the Spirit knows all about our spirit. She does not have to ask probing questions for clues. She will ask us the questions necessary for our perception. Through the Father she knows our life's journey, our heart and mindset. Our Creator, who knows all things about us, reveals to the Spirit our truth. No one can help us understand our emotions or fix what is wrong like our Creator. The One who formed, fashioned, and placed us into existence knowing the challenges, obstacles and situations we would encounter along life's way. The professional therapist has to figure us out. The Creator through the Holy Spirit helps us figure it out for ourselves.

Professional counselors point to people, places and things as the reason for our situations or the influencers of our actions. For some the idea of outside influencers enables them to have an excuse and not take responsibility for their own actions.

The Holy Spirit does not dismiss the people, place and things that affect us but draws our attention on our responses to outside influences. What was done or happened to us is real, however how we react determines the lifelong effect.

So after you have shed your tears and received clarity concerning your emotions then you must talk with the Father, admitting your true feelings. Father, they did me wrong and I am angry. Father, they physically abused me and I am fearful. Father, they took my goodness and walked all over me. Father, they never cared about me but used me, now I feel rejected. Father, they lied and I feel taken advantage of. When you speak the cause and effect of your tears, the Father hears, understands and moves to action. He will dispatch ministering angels to protect you. He will send the Holy Spirit to comfort you and most important He will instruct you on what you must do to prevent and safe guard yourself from future harm. Your Creator knows every cell in your body; your every thought; your situation and circumstances; your heart desires. He promised to mend the brokenhearted; work everything out for your good; give you beauty for ashes; and teach you all things you need to know to be prosperous and healthy. All He asks you to do is to communicate with Him and be honest.   Shedding tears gives us clarity; clarity reveals truth; and truth will set us free.

_8_
Precious Jewels

Our tears are precious jewels that are cultivated through our emotional release. Tears allow us to express feelings which overwhelm us beyond words. They allow us to release harmful experiences which could penetrate our nervous system causing physical diseases and our minds, causing mental anguish. The Creator designed our bodies with tear ducts from which flows supplications, our greatest and strongest emotions.

There is an erroneous myth about tears. _Don't cry is a lie from Satan_. He knows if we don't release negative emotions they will fester inside of us opening a door for his demon squad to attach themselves to our hearts. The heart is so powerful. It is the sustainer of our blood flow continuously pumping throughout our bodies. So vital and important the scriptures tell us, 'God alone knows and judges the heart' _(Jeremiah 17:10 – "I the Lord search the heart, I try the reins, even to give every man according to the fruit of his doings")_.

When we suppress our tears we could leave space for the 'demon squad' or negative spirits called bitterness, malice, hate, rejection, unworthiness, insecurity, anger, fear, frustration, all of which can lead to high blood pressure, dementia, strokes, heart attacks, cancer, depression, suicide, confusion, lack of clarity, physical ailments and limitations. When you cry, YOU release negativity, YOU cast it down, YOU destroy it, and YOU conquer it. When you don't cry it stays with and within you to do as it pleases.

One of the subtle tricks of the enemy is a bitter, mean, angry individual (Christian) who profess happiness or to have the joy of the Lord. They are deceived by the devil. A heart that is pure on the inside will be reflected on the outside. You cannot possess love and happiness if your words and actions are negative.

The best advice I can give you is, "CRY BABY CRY"! DROP A TEAR, use the example of Hannah, cry loud, cry hard, cry long, cry out all the hurt, anger and pain. Cry in the house of God or wherever you may be. Cry unto the Lord for He alone is able to keep you from falling and present you faultless in the presence of your enemies. To be an over comer in life battles, to be purged from pain and negativity, you must submit yourself to **THE POWER OF A TEAR!**

9
The Power of A Tear
SELF APPLICATION

1. Make a list of times or events you did not, were not allowed to; or would not allow yourself to cry.

2. Think about what was going on, what happened:
   - How did it make you feel?
   - What were your thoughts?
   - What was your immediate physical reaction?
   - Why did you decide not to cry?

3. Where did holding back or the blocking of your emotions come from?

4. Why couldn't or can't you cry?

Now that you understand **'The Power of A Tear'**, prepare your environment and your heart for an intimate and emotional talk with The Father. Pray for the release of healing tears. Pray for the joy of experiencing and expressing the emotions He designed for our good. Thank Him for preserving in His vial of remembrance your tears. Thank Him for transforming your tears into precious, genuine, unique one of a kind jewels fashioned by His heart and His hands just for you.

Glossary

Mucin - A glycoprotein constituent of mucus. Mucin is secreted by the salivary glands.

Lipids - Any of a class of organic compounds that are fatty acids or their derivatives and are insoluble in water but soluble in organic solvents. They include many natural oils, waxes, and steroids.

Lysozyme - An enzyme which catalyses the destruction of the cell walls of certain bacteria and occurs notably in tears and egg white.

Lactoferrin - A protein present in milk and other secretions, with bactericidal and iron-binding properties.

Lipocalin –A family of proteins which transport small hydrophobic molecules such as steroids, bilins, retinoids, and lipids.

Lacritin – A secreted protein found in tears and saliva. ...
Some lacritin is produced by the meibomian gland, and by epithelial cells of the conjunctiva and cornea. Together these epithelia comprise much of the lacrimal functional unit (LFU). Dry eye is the most common disease of the LFU.

Immunoglobulin - Any of a class of proteins present in the serum and cells of the immune system, which function as antibodies.

Glucose - A simple sugar which is an important energy source in living organisms and is a component of many carbohydrates.

Urea - A colorless crystalline compound which is the main nitrogenous breakdown product of protein metabolism in mammals and is excreted in urine.

Sodium - The chemical element of atomic number 11, a soft silver-white reactive metal of the alkali metal group.

Potassium - The chemical element of atomic number 19, a soft silvery-white reactive metal of the alkali metal group.

Cerebrum - The principal and most anterior part of the brain in vertebrates, located in the front area of the skull and consisting of two hemispheres, left and right, separated by a fissure. It is responsible for the integration of complex sensory and neural functions and the initiation and coordination of voluntary activity in the body.

Endocrine system - **Relating** to or denoting glands which secrete hormones or other products directly into the blood.

Oxytocin - A hormone released by the pituitary gland that causes increased contraction of the uterus during labor and stimulates the ejection of milk into the ducts of the breasts.

Reference Bibliography

Chapter One
Positive emotions:
http://changingminds.org/explanations/emotions/positiveemotions.
htm

Negative emotions: https://www.learning-mind.com/10-real-
reasons-that-lie-behind-your-negative-emotions/

Tears – Wikipedia - https://en.wikipedia.org/wiki/Tears

Benefits of crying:
https://www.medicalnewstoday.com/articles/319631.php

Chapter Two
King James Study Bible – Nelson King James Version

Definitions:
https://en.oxforddictionaries.com
https://en.wikipedia.org/wiki/Lacritin

ENDORSEMENTS

Our Heavenly Father has provided Sister Corrine E. McCray with the spiritually enlightening roadmap needed for us to fully embrace "God's Call" on His children to become better custodians of the earthly temples He gifted us (1 Corinthians 6:19).

"The Power of A Tear" explores the effects of positive and negative emotions on our spiritual, physical, mental, and family health. Sister Corrine's writing takes the reader on an exploration of Bible-based teachings with medical and scientific background information, which illuminates God's plan and desire for us to be better health and wellness custodians of our bodies, while embracing a life of kingdom fitness, which enables us to perform our Father's work.

Blessings,
Dr. Joseph D. Cohen, DMIN, MDIV, PA-C, CPAAPA, Cary, NC

_____

"*The Power of A Tear*" is a must read regardless of your age, and especially if you believe it's a sign of weakness to cry when feeling hurt or when overwhelmed with happiness. First Lady, Corrine McCray, penned the answer to "why tears are healthy". Her concise writing based on experience and God's voice solidifies the fact that tears are the gateway to Heaven's joy and the perfect escape from emotional bondage.

David Pickett "Helper of All Mankind"
Solution Provider, Shallotte, NC

COVER STORY

All power is in God's hands. The heavy, dark tear drops falling into the hand of God represents negative emotions (fear, anger, depression, etc.). We tend to focus our attention and energy on the dark places which make us feel hopelessness as we struggle.

When the heavy drops fall into the hand of God, they easily slide through His fingers becoming lighter, clear tear drops. When we place our burdens and cares in God's hand, they become lighter and easy to bear. 2 Corinthians 4:17 – "For our light affliction, which is but for a moment, worketh for us a far more exceeding and eternal weight of glory."

Flowing through His cleansing hands, our cares are transformed into blessings. The lighter tear drops accumulate into one large bright ray of light expressing happiness, joy and hope. Happiness pours into a smooth flowing river of refreshing water (cleansing/purification) which touches the lives of others.

Only when we truly give our emotions over to God through the shedding of our tears can He make our burdens light. Releasing to the Father cleanses us because He has power over darkness.

Giving our cares to Him renews our heart, mind and soul.

ABOUT THE AUTHOR

Corrine E. McCray is the wife of Dr. Ronnie L. McCray and they are the proud parents of seven children and eleven grandchildren. They reside in Cary, NC. A native of Washington, DC, the eleventh child of the late Ira and Virgie Day she was raised in the church. Her family faithfully attended services where Corrine developed a love for Sunday School and Bible Study.

The teaching and studying of the Bible created a hunger in her spirit to know, understand and have a relationship with the Father. A child with much imagination, she would boost to friends challenging their superheroes (Batman, Superman, Underdog) to her real life, proven Bible heroes (David, Samson, Elijah and Phillip who outran a chariot).

Corrine loves nature and would walk around her southeast neighborhood visiting neighbors sharing her insight and love for Christ. As she grew older, she walked the streets of Washington meeting people. Her heart filled with compassion as they shared their concerns, fears, and struggles. Realizing many adults were lost and unhappy she shared her confidence in Jesus' love and His ability to help them. During her junior and high school years she was lovingly called Ann Landers because of her gifts of 'help' and 'encouragement'.

A heart of love for people, she equipped herself through studying the Word of God, becoming a passionate teacher, ordained minister and Certified Life and Spiritual Coach. Pastoring with her husband, Corrine focuses on ministering to the natural man and he focuses on the spiritual man. She is motivational speaker, conducts workshops and the Founder of Gracefully Led Life & Spiritual Coaching (GracefullyLed.com). Her motto is "Love gives life".

www.ingramcontent.com/pod-product-compliance
Lightning Source LLC
Chambersburg PA
CBHW070028110426
42741CB00034B/2685